Our Solar System

Written by
Anita Loughrey

Contents

Our Solar System   4
The Milky Way   5
The Sun   6
Mercury   7
Venus   8
Earth   9
Mars   10
The Asteroid Belt   11
Jupiter   12
Saturn   13
Uranus   14
Neptune   15
Pluto   16
Are we alone?   16

Our Solar System

There are eight planets and one star in our solar system.

There are also dwarf planets, moons and comets in our solar system.

The one star in our solar system is the Sun.

The eight planets in our solar system are: Mercury, Venus, Earth, Mars, Jupiter, Saturn, Uranus and Neptune.

The Milky Way

Our solar system is part of a large galaxy called the Milky Way. There are more than 400 billion stars in the Milky Way. There are billions of other solar systems in the Milky Way too.

The Sun

The Sun is at the centre of our solar system. The Sun is a star. It is very big and very hot. All the planets in our solar system go around the Sun. We say that they orbit the Sun.

Mercury

Mercury is the planet closest to the Sun. It is the smallest planet in our solar system.

The surface of the planet Mercury is dry and covered with craters.

Mercury is about 50 million kilometres from the Sun.

Venus

Venus is the second planet from the Sun. It is the hottest planet and also the brightest planet in our solar system. Venus is so bright that you can see it from Earth during the daytime.

The surface of Venus is covered by thick gases.

Venus is about 108 million kilometres from the Sun.

Earth

Earth is the third planet from the Sun. It is the only planet that we know has life on it. It is also the only planet to have liquid water – and it is our home.

Earth is about 150 million kilometres from the Sun.

Mars

Mars is the fourth planet from the Sun.
It is known as the red planet.
The surface of Mars is covered with red rocks, dust and soil. Mars has mountains and valleys like Earth.
Mars is about 230 million kilometres from the Sun.

The Asteroid Belt

Our solar system is divided into two parts by the asteroid belt. The two parts are called the inner solar system and the outer solar system.

The asteroid belt is made up of hundreds of thousands of rocks and asteroids orbiting the Sun.

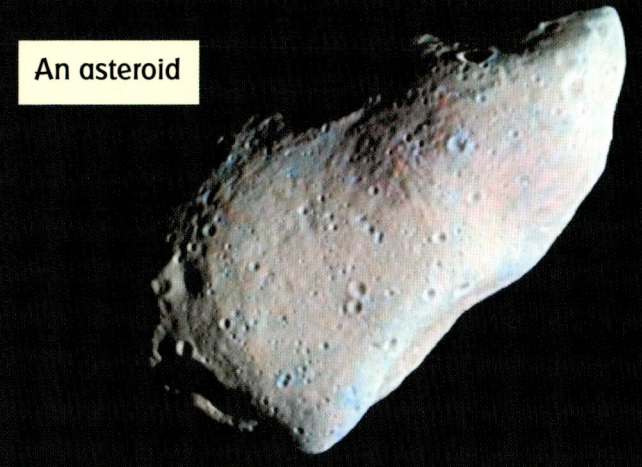

An asteroid

Jupiter

Jupiter is the fifth planet from the Sun. It is the largest planet in our solar system.

Most of Jupiter is made up of gas. We call Jupiter a gas giant. Jupiter has more than 64 moons.

The planet is about 778 million kilometres from the Sun.

Saturn

Saturn is the sixth planet from the Sun. It is a gas giant. Saturn is the second largest planet in the solar system.

Saturn has rings. The rings are made from ice.

Saturn is about 1.4 billion kilometres from the Sun.

Uranus

Uranus is the seventh planet from the Sun. It cannot be seen from Earth without a telescope.

Uranus is a gas giant. It has 27 moons.

Uranus is about 3 billion kilometres from the Sun.

Neptune

Neptune is the eighth planet from the Sun. Neptune is the third largest planet in the solar system. It is a gas giant, and has the strongest winds of all the planets.

Neptune is about 4.5 billion kilometres from the Sun.

Pluto

Until 2006 Pluto was called the ninth planet. Now Pluto is no longer counted as a planet because it is too small. Now we call it a dwarf planet.

Pluto is about 5 billion kilometres from the Sun.

Pluto

Are we alone?

Scientists are finding planets outside our solar system. These planets orbit other stars in the Milky Way.

Some people think that there are living things on these planets. But nobody knows; the planets are too far away to see!